UNF*CK YOUR LIFE LIKE
VIKRAM

VIKAS SHARMA

ISBN
Hardcase 979-8-89610-327-1
Paperback 979-8-89556-383-0

Dedication

To my father, who taught me the power of stories long before I ever picked up a pen. Though you are no longer here to read these words, your wisdom and love continue to guide me with every page I write.

This book is for you, Dad. Thank you for always believing in my dreams, even when they were just whispers in the wind. Your memory lives on in every story I tell.

Contents

ACKNOWLEDGEMENTS

This book would not exist without the unwavering love and support of those closest to me.

To my parents, thank you for your constant guidance, for always believing in me, and for nurturing my imagination from the very beginning. Your wisdom has shaped not just this book, but the person I am today.

To my incredible spouse Neha, your faith in me and your gentle push to finally bring this book into the world have been invaluable. Your encouragement gave me the courage to take this step, and for that, I am forever grateful.

And to my sister Minakashi and brother-in-law Jagat, your encouragement and support have meant the world to me. Thank you for always being there, cheering me on through every challenge and triumph.

This book is as much yours as it is mine. Thank you all, from the bottom of my heart.

PROLOGUE

Life has a funny way of sucker-punching you when you least expect it. Meet Vikram, just your average middle-class Indian bloke, brimming with dreams and boundless energy. He kicked off well, but life, as it often does, sent him careening off-course with a series of questionable decisions and some lousy timing. Vikram, like many of us, was destined to learn the beautiful and painful lessons of life's hard knocks. Setbacks came and went, but his never-say-die attitude allowed him to confront every challenge with a defiant smile. Eventually, he found his life's purpose amidst the chaos.

Vikram, once a timid schoolboy, wouldn't dare speak a single word in public, let alone face the dreaded socialising with the opposite sex. The mere thought of addressing the school assembly made him so nervous that he once vomited after uttering a single line. That's how painfully shy he was. In the beginning, he was so inconspicuous that teachers regularly demanded his ID. But, as fate would have it, college transformed him into a social butterfly. He became so popular that even professors and girls couldn't resist his charm. His honesty, determination, and willpower were the stuff of legends. Success seemed inevitable, but life had its own ideas. After earning his B.Tech degree, Vikram's thirst for knowledge led him to Bangalore, where he secured admission to a prestigious college. Life appeared to be taking shape, with promising opportunities on the horizon. However, just as everything seemed sorted, a dark cloud loomed over the country in the form of a depression wave, leading to a dearth of jobs. Vikram, though, found a ray of hope, an opportunity that might not have matched his qualifications but cracked open the door of a world-renowned organisation. He put his heart and soul into it, climbing the ladder rung by rung.

Once again, life took on a twist. Restlessness crept in, and dissatisfaction seeped into his days. Then came the "India Against Corruption" movement, a political earthquake that rattled Vikram to his core. He felt a calling—a duty to serve his country. So, he abandoned his cushy job and moved to Delhi, determined to prepare for the civil services.

But that too was a fleeting aspiration. Gradually, it dissolved into thin air, and Vikram found himself back in the corporate world, navigating the roller coaster of ups and downs. Typical Vikram. Life, however, had a few more cards up its sleeve. An opportunity beckoned Vikram to relocate to Singapore, with a beautiful woman as his life partner. He felt on top of the world, not realising that this decision would be the pivoting point for an unforeseen turn of events. Yet, they say, when life serves you a setback, you're left with two choices: become bitter or become better. Vikram chose the latter, embarking on a journey to discover his true purpose after the most devastating setback of his life.

And so begins the unconventional tale of Vikram, a man who learned that life's lessons are often written in the ink of adversity.

Chapter One

WHEN THE UNEXPECTED BECOMES THE UNFORGETTABLE

"Success is not the absence of failure; it's the persistence through failure."

The day Vikram had been waiting for—actually, obsessing over—finally arrived. He'd always dreamt of this moment, but when the call came from the HR department of his dream company, it felt surreal. He answered with a mix of excitement and disbelief, his mind flashing back to his awkward, introverted teenage years in a small, unremarkable town.

Here is the honest truth: Vikram's journey wasn't some grand, effortless climb to success. It was more of a messy, stumbling ascent. He went from being the shy kid who wouldn't dare speak up in class, to a young man trying to figure out life's crapshoot. Back in school, Vikram was a short, wiry guy with a complexion that made him blend into the background. Socially, he was a disaster. He'd take a thousand extra steps just to avoid a conversation with a group of girls. Public speaking?

Let's just say it involved a lot of stomach-churning moments and, at one point, actual vomit. It was a hell of a contrast to the confident guy he hoped to become, and those school years felt like a series of unfortunate events.

Then came college—his big shot. Suddenly, he was in a place where being good at something actually meant something. Academics? Nailed it. Extracurriculars? Got those too. But then, reality hit. By his third year, the job market was a mess. His peers were freaking out, and Vikram, who was supposed to be this cool, calm dude preparing for his Master's, was a bundle of nerves. After two tries at the GATE exam and a whole lot of stress, he got into a prestigious Bioinformatics programme in Bangalore. Exciting, right? Except his mom was about to have a meltdown over him moving so far away. His dad, however, was the rock who understood why this mattered and stood by him. As Vikram packed his bags—four of them, because why not?—his mom made sweets and his dad gave him that look that said, "This is a big deal."

The hostel was a far cry from luxury, situated in a quaint village with local shops. The building was a melting pot of students from all over India, and Vikram was assigned to the boys' floor. Enter Akash Tyagi from Meerut, who knocked on Vikram's door with his father in tow. Akash was a few years older, a small-town guy with a heart as big as his wisdom. He wasn't just a friend; he was the kind of mentor who'd tell you straight up when you're screwing up.

The first year at the institute was like being thrown into the deep end of a pool full of genius. Vikram swam hard to keep up, fuelled by the pressure and his own burning desire to succeed. But, oh boy, the climax was a real punch in the gut. The 2008 financial crisis hit, and suddenly, the job market was a wasteland. Companies pulled out, and Vikram was left with one measly internship offer from a company associated with the institute. He impressed the recruiter, but true to form, he decided to turn it down, holding out for his dream company. His friends got offers and left for Diwali, while Vikram sat alone in the hostel, mired in regret.

There he was, sitting on the terrace, the weight of his decision crushing him. Why the hell hadn't he taken the offer? The guilt was gnawing at him until Akash, who had already secured a job but chose to stay behind, showed up. He listened as Vikram poured out his fears and doubts, offering advice that was both practical and hopeful. "Reapply," Akash said, "because sometimes life throws curveballs, and you've got to swing for the fences."

So Vikram did just that. He reapplied, and his inbox eventually pinged with an internship offer. The joy was palpable. He called Akash and said, "Bro, let's book our tickets home for Diwali."

This marked the beginning of Vikram's corporate journey—an unexpected twist on a path he thought he'd mapped out perfectly. It wasn't the glamorous entry his friends and family had imagined, but it was his. It was a testament to sticking it out through the crap and finding a way forward. And as Vikram looked ahead, he knew one thing for sure: his journey, with all its messy detours, had made him resilient enough to handle whatever came next.

16 ◆ *UNF*CK YOUR LIFE LIKE VIKRAM*

crap and finding a way forward. And as Vikram looked ahead, he knew one thing for sure: his journey, with all its messy detours, had made him resilient enough to handle whatever came next.

Chapter Two

LEAP OF FAITH

"Sometimes, you have gotta risk it all to discover what truly matters."

So, Vikram kicked off his career as an intern, and his "I've got this" attitude wasn't just a show. Within three months, he had morphed into a full-time employee while his colleagues were still playing catch-up. It was impressive, but Vikram was only getting started. In a year, he notched up two promotions, making the office buzz with gossip about the new star. Meanwhile, he was juggling a distance MBA, living the dream, or so it seemed.

But life has a cruel sense of humour. Out of nowhere, an old college buddy dropped a job offer in IT. Vikram, who thrived on diving headfirst into challenges, thought, "Why not?" He took the leap. Walking into his new IT gig felt like stepping onto another planet—sprawling campuses, vibrant cafeterias, endless free coffee, and gyms that could rival five-star resorts. It was a far cry from his previous life in life sciences. Initially, his lack of formal IT training was a roadblock, but Vikram's stubborn determination and his new team's support helped him climb the ranks again. Enter Devvrat—a guy so effortlessly charming he could sell sand in a desert. Within a short span of time, Devvrat became more than just a colleague; he was a friend who would ride the emotional roller coaster with Vikram.

Everything seemed to be falling into place – new job, MBA almost done, and a promising six-month European assignment. Life was good, right? Wrong. Just as everything seemed perfect, Vikram hit a snag. Appraisal time rolled around, and he noticed he hadn't received an invite. Confused and a bit annoyed, he went to his manager's office.

"Hey, can I come in?" Vikram asked, trying to sound casual but clearly irritated.

The manager waved him in. "What's up?"

"Seems like everyone's got their appraisal meetings scheduled except me. What's going on?" Vikram's patience was wearing thin.

The manager hesitated. "Oh, right. Since you joined in December, and our policy has shifted to anniversary-based appraisals, you'll have to wait until December for yours."

Vikram's frustration bubbled. "But I was promised my package would be adjusted in the next cycle. This doesn't seem fair."

The manager's response was as dry as the Sahara. "I get it, but this policy is out of my control. Sorry."

Vikram left, seething. He wasn't mad at his boss, but the whole situation felt like a raw deal. Fuelled by frustration and an impulsive streak, he decided to quit. His traits—honesty, drive, and, let's face it, a tendency to act without thinking—came into play again.

He updated his resume and dove into the job market. Lucky break: he found three excellent opportunities and chose to work for a top-tier company. His first day at this new job was a sensory overload—vivid walls, gourmet coffee, and a PlayStation in the break room. HR greeted him with all the fanfare of a rock star. Among the new faces was Samrat, a guy who looked like he walked straight out of a rock concert. Long, curly hair, denim, and a Linkin Park T-shirt—Samrat was unapologetically himself. Beneath his nonconformist exterior was a sharp mind and a passion for coding. He quickly became a lifelong friend.

So, life was rolling along—new friends, a stimulating job, and the MBA nearly complete. But Vikram was not one for comfort zones. When the Anna movement—a massive anti-corruption protest led by Anna Hazare— hit, it struck a chord with him. He even fasted for a day in solidarity. This movement reignited his old dream of serving his country. Although he had once wanted to join the Indian Army, family expectations had led him astray. Now, he decided it was time to chase that dream. After some soul-searching and talks with his loved ones, Vikram chose to pursue the UPSC exam with the goal of becoming an IAS officer. Big change, bigger challenge.

He shared his plan with Samrat and other close friends. They rallied behind him, and Vikram plunged into intense study. His life became a regimented routine:

office by day, study by night, classes on weekends. It was a grind, but he found a new sense of purpose in it.

When the UPSC preliminary exam day came, Vikram felt ready. But when the results were released, his name was nowhere to be found. The disappointment was a gut punch. He called Samrat, trying to mask his frustration.

Samrat, always the realist, met him at their favourite tea spot. "Look, man, cracking UPSC is brutal, especially with a full-time job. I've seen your hustle, and if this attempt didn't pan out, don't sweat it. There's always another shot. Maybe consider taking a sabbatical to focus on this fully."

The idea struck a chord. With his father's blessing, Vikram decided to go for it. The next day, he asked HR and his director for a sabbatical. He initially requested eight months but faced resistance. So, Vikram, true to form, made another impulsive decision – he quit his well-paying job to follow his passion.

A month later, at Bangalore railway station, Samrat waved Vikram off as he boarded the Rajdhani Express. As Vikram settled into his journey, he reflected on his choices, his past decisions, and the uncertain future that lay ahead.

Chapter Three

QUITTING, DREAMING, AND THE ROAD AHEAD

"Sometimes, the bravest decision you can make is to admit that a dream no longer serves your purpose."

Vikram's return home was a mixed bag, and I'm not just talking about the luggage. His mother was overjoyed to have him back after seven long years, but she couldn't shake her worries about his decision to leave a well-paying job. Competing with half a million people for a thousand government positions? That's not just ambitious; it's borderline crazy. Still, she knew his potential and prayed for him like only a mother could.

After a week of unwinding in Patiala, Vikram reached out to Gautam, a friend from his UPSC prep days in Bangalore. Gautam was the kind of guy who traded in a cushy IT job for a gruelling UPSC prep grind—talk about going from the frying pan into the fire.

"Hey Vikram, how's it going? Long time no talk," Gautam's voice was a blast from the past.

"Yeah, I'm good, Cheete. What's up with you and how's the prep?" Vikram responded.

They had this quirky nickname 'Cheete' for each other back in Bangalore.

"Solid, man. I'm back in my hometown now and planning to head to Delhi for further studies. You should come by this weekend. I will show you around and help you find a place," Gautam suggested.

"Sounds good. I will give you a call before I head out. You just keep doing your thing," Vikram agreed. With that, he ended the call, leaving Gautam eagerly awaiting their reunion.

On Sunday, Vikram boarded a bus to Delhi. Ninety minutes later, he emerged at Kashmere Gate and hopped onto the Metro, heading towards Rajendra Nagar, the heartland of UPSC dreams. Gautam was waiting at the station, and they drove straight into Delhi's street food scene. Vikram listened intently to Gautam's tales, knowing he was about to live this life himself.

Gautam, staying at his uncle's place, was well-versed in the art of room hunting. They scoured the notice boards at a coaching institute and found a promising room rental ad. Vikram was hesitant; he was used to a solitary 1 BHK apartment back in Bangalore and wasn't thrilled about shared spaces.

Life in Rajendra Nagar was no walk in the park. The small, poorly ventilated room on the top floor was a far cry from Vikram's previous luxurious setup. But he was determined to make it work.

After settling on the room, Vikram needed to enrol in Sociology classes, his chosen subject for the UPSC mains. He signed up for Professor Subash Mohapatra's afternoon batch. His first class was a sensory overload—200 students, six AC units, and a stuffy room that made him feel like he was suffocating. He found a seat and started reading the news, trying to drown out the discomfort.

Suddenly, a gentle tap on his shoulder jolted him. He turned to see Dipali, a vision of enchantment with her fair complexion, mesmerising brown eyes, and dark hair cascading like a midnight waterfall. For a moment, everything else faded. Her request for a pen felt like a prelude to something much bigger.

"Excuse me, do you have an extra pen? I forgot mine," she asked, her voice carrying a hint of serendipity.

Caught off guard but trying to play it cool, Vikram handed her the pen. "Yeah, I have one," he managed, his heart doing a little dance. That simple exchange felt like it was scripted by fate.

Their initial connection sparked a series of coffee and dinner dates. One day, during a festival break when the institute was closed, Vikram mustered the courage to ask Dipali out. To his surprise, she agreed. They had a hearty breakfast at The Indian Coffee House, a place with a British-era charm that Dipali loved. As they walked through the park, Vikram decided to use an old trick that had never failed him.

"Hey Dipali, mind if I check out your hands?" Vikram asked with a sly grin.

Dipali laughed, "Oh, trying to play the palmist, are we?".

Vikram grinned back, "You caught me. I dabbled in palm reading during my B.Tech days. So, what do your hands say?"

Dipali extended her hand, and Vikram, armed with a bit of Facebook sleuthing, shared some intriguing details about her past. Her curiosity piqued, and she leaned in, eager to hear more. Vikram mixed in some generic horoscope-style statements to keep it interesting. After the park and the palm reading, Vikram walked Dipali to her PG. They hugged, and to his shock, she gave him a quick goodnight kiss before darting inside. Vikram stood there, stunned, before heading back to his room.

Six months of intense studying and occasional dates had brought them closer. Then came the day Vikram had been working towards—the prelim exam. It was a bright Delhi morning, and Vikram set out early, determined to arrive at least 30 minutes before the exam. He got there a full 45 minutes early, and the exam centre was already buzzing with anxious students.

The exam itself went well—or so Vikram thought. The results were still two months away, and he decided to take a break. Returning to town after a week's rest, Vikram found that most of his friends had left for their hometowns, but Dipali had vanished without a word. Her abrupt departure left him confused and hurt, disrupting his focus for another week.

But life doesn't wait, and Vikram resumed his preparation for the UPSC mains. This time, he felt a growing disconnection from the world of UPSC. The more he studied, the more he questioned whether he was cut out for this. Doubts crept in about whether he should have left his well-paying job for this path. His inner turmoil grew as he awaited the results.

Then, one night, a call from Gautam shattered his restless thoughts. Gautam had cleared the prelims, but when Vikram mentioned his roll number, the mood shifted. Vikram hadn't made the cut. That night, he sat on the terrace, staring into the darkness, feeling the weight of his setback. The next day, he broke the news to his parents, who were sympathetic yet determined not to let him wallow.

Professor Mohapatra, noticing Vikram's shift in demeanour, pulled him aside. "Everything okay?" he asked, his tone betraying genuine concern.

Vikram, trying to put on a brave face, assured him he was fine, but Mohapatra saw through it. "Sometimes," the professor said, "you need to know when to pivot. If UPSC isn't the path, there are other ways to serve."

Those words hit home. Vikram realised that quitting didn't mean failure—it meant choosing a new direction.

He began exploring job opportunities, ready to embrace a new path. Just as he was discussing his options, a call from his former organisation's HR changed everything.

"Hey Vikram, how's it going?" The HR voice was familiar, and the question felt oddly comforting.

"I'm doing well, thanks. How about you?" Vikram asked, intrigued.

"I'm good too. We haven't filled your position yet. Interested in coming back?" HR offered.

Vikram's decision was about to undergo a profound transformation. He'd just realised that sometimes, the path you think is closed can open in ways you never expected.

Chapter Four

THE UNEXPECTED INTERVIEW

"Embracing the Curveballs Life Throws"

Vikram felt like he'd just pulled himself out of quicksand. When the HR department called with the job offer, it was like stumbling upon a lifeline after flailing in a sea of disappointment. The chance for redemption was too precious to pass up. He grabbed at it, without even bothering to check the compensation. It wasn't about the money right now; it was about proving he wasn't just a series of failures. The past misadventure with the UPSC had left him feeling like he'd been wrestling with shadows, and this offer was a flicker of light in that dark struggle.

The HR rep seemed equally relieved. "That's great to hear, Vikram. We're thrilled to have you," HR said, diving into the administrative nitty-gritty and travel plans.

"Thanks a lot for this," Vikram replied, his shoulders already feeling lighter. Hanging up the phone, he felt a rush of gratitude—like the universe had given him a second shot at life. The next day, the admin called to finalise travel details.

"Welcome back, Vikram!" the admin's enthusiasm was contagious. "Got your logistics sorted. It's fantastic to have you back."

"Thanks, buddy. We talked yesterday, and I'm excited to be in Bangalore. Just let me know the travel details," Vikram said, adding a touch of humour to lighten the mood.

"Can't wait to see if the city's as glamorous as the movies make it out to be."

"Got it, Vikram. I'll send you the details by this evening. Can you confirm your email?" the admin asked eagerly.

Vikram provided his email and other necessary details. After sometime he received an email with his flight tickets attached, he looked at the flight tickets with a mix of relief and excitement. It felt surreal to be holding this second chance in his hands.

Departure day came, and the evening sky was casting a wintry chill. As Vikram walked through the airport, he saw a valet holding a placard with his name—a touch of movie magic that made him feel unexpectedly special. He introduced himself, and the valet tried to take his luggage, but Vikram insisted on handling it himself. Old habits die hard; he was all about self-reliance.

The drive to the hotel took a gruelling hour and a half, thanks to Bangalore's infamous traffic. Vikram tried to strike up a conversation with the driver, but the driver's nods and smiles made it clear he wasn't comfortable with Hindi and English. Vikram, ever the optimist, decided a quick nap was the better option.

"Wake up, sir! We've arrived at the hotel," the driver's voice jolted Vikram from his nap. He thanked the driver, tipped him generously, and headed into the hotel's reception area.

It was 8:00 PM, and Vikram was exhausted. He called a few friends in Bangalore to let them know about his arrival and ordered dinner. The plan was simple: get a good night's rest and prepare for the big day ahead. At precisely 9:00 AM the next morning, Vikram arrived at the office. The receptionist greeted him with a familiar face.

"Hey, Vikram. How's it going? Hope you slept well," HR said, extending a firm handshake.

"I'm good. The flight was fine, thanks. How about you?" Vikram replied, shaking HR's hand.

"Doing well. Ready to get started?" HR asked, catching Vikram off guard with their straightforward approach. The tone was a bit too blunt, making Vikram wonder if something was amiss.

Vikram had expected the usual interview process, but this felt different. The director questions his experiences and future plans, putting Vikram at ease. Yet, as the conversation abruptly ended, Vikram's internal alarm bells went off. He sensed something was off and thanked the director before heading back to HR.

Thanks for coming, Vikram. We'll be in touch with the next steps," HR said with a practiced HR tone. He thanked HR and called his friend Samrat.

"Hey, man, just wrapped up the interview. Not feeling too optimistic. What's your schedule like?"

"Let's catch up later," Vikram admitted, his voice betraying a hint of disappointment.

"Just took half the day off. Let's hit Aunty ka Dhaba—are you in?" Samrat replied, sounding like a lifeline himself.

Vikram agreed, feeling a bit raw from the earlier encounter with the director. When Samrat arrived, their conversation turned to potential outcomes and the local food. Just as they were discussing what might come next, Vikram's phone rang again. It was HR.

"Hey, Vikram. Hope you're well. We've received your feedback and are putting things on hold for now. We'll let you know in a few days. We'll also book your return flight to Delhi. Is tomorrow morning okay with you?"

Vikram read between the lines. Experience had taught him that this was likely a polite brush-off. He wasn't ready to give up just yet. He braced himself for this, Politely refused the offer for a return flight to Delhi and thanked HR once more.

Samrat, sensing Vikram's unease, tried to lift his spirits with encouragement. Vikram, momentarily disheartened, found a spark of resolve.

"Yeah, you're right," Vikram said, his eyes lighting up with renewed determination. "I'm not giving up. Let's see what comes next."

Samrat was impressed by Vikram's newfound resilience. Despite the setback, his friend had found the strength to face another challenge. Their conversation shifted back to more immediate concerns—like indulging in Paneer Tikka, Chole bhatura, and Gulab Jamun.

Chapter Five

FROM SETBACK TO SOARING: VIKRAM'S TRIUMPH

"When life knocks you down, rise stronger."

"Let's plan after work. I'll swing by your hotel; we'll check out and head to my place. You can crash there, get ready for your interview," Samrat said, finishing his bhatura with a satisfied grin, as if it was the last thing that mattered in the world.

"Sounds good," Vikram replied, trying to sound casual but failing to hide the flicker of desperation in his eyes.

"Let me pack, and we'll leave together in the evening."

And just like that, they each trudged off, each wrapped up in their own brand of existential dread.

When Vikram showed up at Samrat's place, he was greeted by a home that felt like a safe harbour amidst his stormy sea of rejections. Samrat's parents had laid out a spread that could only be described as gastronomic therapy. The table was laden with comfort food that practically screamed, "We know you're stressed, so here's some love on a plate." The warmth from the food and the family wrapped around Vikram like a blanket on a cold night.

As they sat down to eat, Samrat's father, a man whose stoic demeanour made him seem like he'd seen it all, spoke with such earnestness that Vikram's own father's absence felt like a fresh wound. Samrat's mother, with her knowing glances and gentle encouragement, made Vikram feel like he was part of their family's emotional support system.

Yet, despite this unexpected oasis of kindness, Vikram couldn't shake the gnawing anxiety. Confidence? Sure, he had a pinch of that. But it was tangled up with a mountain of self-doubt. The next morning, he threw himself into a frenzied campaign to find a job. He sent his resume out like confetti at a New Year's Eve party—everywhere and anywhere. His drive wasn't just determination; it was pure, unfiltered desperation.

There's this cliché about how "When you set your eyes on something, the universe conspires to help you." Well, Vikram had a few interviews lined up in December. A miracle? Maybe. But it felt more like a tease. The rejections came in faster than he could process them. One minute, he was making it to the final rounds; the next, he was face-down in the dirt, rejected. Hope was becoming an elusive ghost, mocking him from the shadows.

During this rollercoaster of misery, his friends were his rock. They kept reminding him that setbacks are just temporary—and that's the kind of advice that's easier to give than to live by. One day, his frustration hit an all-time high. He wore his irritation like a medal of honour, letting everyone see his irritation without apology. Samrat, ever the intuitive friend, dragged Vikram out for tea.

The tea shop was a tiny haven, and the aroma of chai mixed with the warmth of the place was like a gentle slap to the face—a reminder that life could be good, even if it felt like it was falling apart. Over chai and veg puffs, Samrat shared stories of people who had climbed out of their own personal pits of despair and made something of themselves. These stories weren't just motivational fluff; they were the kind of raw, gritty accounts that made Vikram's own struggles seem like a bump in the road.

Then, as they were diving into their conversation, Vikram's phone rang. It was the HR from Smart Digital Solutions, the tech company in Chandigarh. They wanted to offer him the job of Senior Software Engineer. The words barely registered as Vikram's mind went into overdrive. His heart raced, and he stared at the phone as if it were some sort of cruel joke. "Thanks, ma'am, for the offer. I'm outside right now. I'll check it as soon as I get home and let you know," he managed to stammer.

Samrat, catching the dazed look on Vikram's face, asked, "What's up? What did they say?"

"I got the job!"Vikram blurted out, his voice cracking with a mix of disbelief and sheer, unfiltered joy. His fist pumped the air, and for the first time in ages, he felt like the universe wasn't out to screw him over.

Without missing a beat, Samrat ordered a chocolate truffle cake, because if you can't celebrate with cake, are you even celebrating? As they indulged in the rich sweetness, they talked through the job offer—Chandigarh, the dream city, closer to home, and the chance to start fresh. Each reason Vikram listed felt like a weight lifted off his shoulders. He called his father, and hearing his dad's voice crack with pride was the final piece of reassurance he needed.

He organised a small gathering to thank his friends for sticking by him and gave parting gifts to Samrat and his family. His gratitude was raw and heartfelt, a genuine thank you to those who had been his emotional lifeline.

The departure day finally arrived. At the airport, Samrat stood by Vikram, their bond unshaken by the separation. With hugs and promises to catch up soon, Vikram boarded the flight to Chandigarh. As the plane took off, he looked out the window, the city lights below twinkling like tiny beacons of hope. It wasn't just a new job; it was a new chapter, written with resilience and the unrelenting support of friends and family.

Chapter Six

FROM AWKWARD BEGINNINGS TO UNCERTAIN ENDINGS

"In the dance of love, sometimes the steps are uncertain, but it's the rhythm of the heart that leads us forward."

On a crisp Chandigarh morning, with winter's bite in the air, Vikram stepped out of the airport, bundled in his jacket. He was waiting for Sandy, his friend known for his resourcefulness and extensive network. Sandy, affectionately nicknamed Jugadu, was there to welcome Vikram. Despite Vikram's respect for Sandy, he hesitated to stay in Sandy's modest hostel when his new job offered a week's stay in a luxurious 4-star hotel.

As Vikram settled into his new office, he found himself surrounded by friendly colleagues and, inevitably, attractive coworkers. The days flew by, blending work with Sandy's jovial circle of friends. But an unexpected challenge soon emerged: Vikram needed accommodation as a bachelor. After several unsuccessful attempts, Sandy, now exasperated, insisted Vikram stay at the hostel. Reluctantly, Vikram agreed. The next day, the seasoned team lead found himself enrolled in a basic computer course and sharing a hostel room—thanks to Sandy's persuasive prowess.

Life in Chandigarh became a whirlwind of new experiences. Vikram relished the camaraderie of Sandy's vibrant group and his colleagues. However, his routine was disrupted one day when he lost track of time in a spirited game of table tennis. His phone buzzed incessantly on his desk—ten missed calls from Devvrat, a friend whose urgency was palpable. Unease gripped Vikram as he dialled Devvrat's number.

"Hey bro, all okay?" Vikram asked, his concern evident.

"Yeah, I'm good. Sorry for the multiple calls; I've got some exciting news," Devvrat replied, his voice a mix of anticipation and eagerness.

"Alright, spill it! What's the big news?" Vikram's curiosity was piqued.

"Remember my elder brother? You were a witness on his marriage certificate," Devrat said, a slight grin in his voice.

"Yeah, I remember him," Vikram replied, trying to recall the details.

"Well, he is starting a new company in Singapore and wants you to join as a project manager. Interested?" Devvrat asked, his tone direct and hopeful.

Vikram was stunned by the offer. After a brief pause, he masked his excitement and replied, "Congratulations,

Devvrat. That's fantastic news. Please give my best to your brother. I need some time to think it over. I will get back to you."

"Absolutely, take your time. My brother will call you this weekend to discuss his vision. It's a great opportunity. We'll catch up later," Devvrat said before ending the call.

Those ten minutes sparked a whirlwind of thoughts in Vikram's mind. Just a month ago, he was jobless; now, he was considering relocating to Singapore. It was a tough decision, but Vikram decided to follow his heart. He shared the news with his parents, who supported him while advising caution and reminding him about the prospect of finding a suitable match. Vikram nodded in agreement, and his parents quickly began the search for a potential partner.

One weekend, as Vikram relaxed with friends, his phone chimed with his mother's call. He hesitated but answered, anticipating the usual conversation.

"Hey, Mom," Vikram greeted, expecting her enthusiasm.

"Hi, Vikram," she replied, her voice animated. "I just got back from a relative's wedding. Guess what? Your distant uncle brought up something interesting. We might have found someone special for you! I was blown away by her photos. She's beautiful with a radiant charm. I can't wait for you to see her!"

Vikram chuckled at his mom's excitement.

"Really, Mom? That's great! Tell me more."

"Well, her family is reputable, and our astrologer gave a thumbs up for compatibility. Your dad will send you her picture on WhatsApp. Take your time, but if you like her, we're set for the next steps—meetings, discussions, the whole shebang! I have a good feeling about this," she said, her enthusiasm palpable.

As Vikram listened, he felt a surge of excitement. The prospect of a potential life partner seemed more real and exhilarating. "I can not wait to see her picture, Mom. Let's see what destiny has in store."

A few minutes later, his dad sent two WhatsApp messages with photos of his prospective bride. She was lovely, her smile infectious, dressed in casual attire—a stark contrast to the typical polished alliance photos. Vikram's curiosity was piqued. He called his dad.

"Hey Dad, I saw the photos. She seems nice. I would like to get to know her better," Vikram said, hiding his true feelings.

"Alright, I will have your mom contact your uncle and arrange the details," his dad replied. "By the way, Vikram, I am curious. You are usually selective and don't show interest this quickly. What's different this time?"

Vikram was taken aback. "Oh, nothing, Dad. Mom mentioned this alliance came from the uncle's side, so I thought I should respond promptly to avoid any delays." His dad sensed there was more but chose not to press further and agreed to facilitate the next steps.

Days later, Vikram received an unexpected call from an unknown number. Hesitant but curious, he answered.

"Hey Vikram, it's Poonam. How's it going?" Her cheerful voice radiated through the phone.

"Oh, hey Poonam! I'm good. How about you?" Vikram replied, trying to sound casual.

"Same old, you know. Dodging marriage proposals and all," Poonam chuckled; her headstrong attitude evident even over the phone.

Vikram laughed nervously. "Yeah, tell me about it. It's like everyone's in a rush to get married, right?"

"Exactly! Who needs that kind of pressure?" Poonam's tone softened, finding a kindred spirit in Vikram.

"I get it. Everyone expects us to have our lives figured out by now," Vikram said, sensing a connection.

Poonam laughed, easing the tension. "Right? Can we just enjoy life without worrying about settling down?"

"Exactly! So, what do you enjoy doing in your free time, Poonam?" Vikram asked, shifting the conversation to personal interests.

"Well, I love photography, hence all those photos you've seen. And I'm trying to master cooking without burning the kitchen down," Poonam said with a laugh.

Vikram chuckled. "That's impressive. I'm terrible in the kitchen. Maybe you could teach me a thing or two sometime?"

Poonam's laughter was warm and inviting. "Sure, Vikram. Just be ready for a few burnt dishes and blurry photos. It's all part of the learning process."

Their conversation flowed effortlessly, revealing shared interests and values. Beneath Poonam's confident exterior was an underlying reluctance. She had hoped to make a poor impression, but as they continued to talk, a genuine connection began to form.

They agreed to meet in person. Vikram travelled to Pune, his heart filled with curiosity and uncertainty. Throughout the journey, he pondered Poonam's enigmatic behaviour and felt an inexplicable attraction—a yearning to know her better. Their first meeting in Pune was awkward but significant. They visited local attractions, with Poonam's moods swinging unpredictably. Vikram noticed her warmth, her flashes of temper, and her resistance to tradition.

The trip left Vikram perplexed but intrigued. He grappled with his emotions, questioning if there was something deeper between them. As their late-night conversations continued, they debated passionately on topics like women's rights, challenging each other's perspectives. Despite their differences, Vikram felt a magnetic pull towards her.

One day, after a particularly intense debate, Vikram felt a powerful urge. He had to call her, despite her earlier aloofness. He dialled her number, hoping to bridge any gaps.

"Hey Vikram, how are you?" Poonam's voice was warm; her curiosity genuine.

"Good," Vikram replied, nervous yet determined. "I was thinking maybe we could give this another shot. I find our conversations intriguing and would like to see where they lead."

Poonam paused; her expression guarded. Vikram's vulnerability and transparency eventually softened her demeanour.

"I appreciate your honesty, Vikram," Poonam said, her voice warming. "I felt something was off before too. Let's give it another try and see where it goes."

A sense of relief washed over Vikram. He decided to continue their conversation, allowing their connection to develop naturally.

Their relationship, marked by ups and downs and simmering tensions, felt extraordinary. As days turned into weeks, Vikram's attachment to Poonam deepened. He grappled with his emotions, unsure if it was love, infatuation, or the beginning of something transformative. His decision to meet Poonam's family once more opened a new chapter in their relationship, one that would test their connection and reveal whether it could withstand life's unpredictable challenges.

Days turned into weeks, and before he knew it, Vikram had said "yes" to marriage. Excitement and apprehension filled him as he prepared to leave for his new job in Singapore. The courtship period continued, filled with fights, compromises, and a deepening connection. It was a rollercoaster, but Vikram and Poonam weathered the storms, emerging stronger. Their wedding day arrived, and amidst the celebrations, Vikram pondered the enigmatic woman he had chosen to spend his life with. As they embarked on this new journey together, Vikram's mind was filled with questions about the future—questions only time would answer.

Chapter Seven

THE STORMY KARWA CHAUTH

"Amidst the glow of Karwa Chauth, a storm of conflicting beliefs and emotions brews."

In the chaos of Singapore, where skyscrapers flirt with the clouds, Vikram and Poonam set off on a journey that would test their relationship's very core. Their love story began with excitement and passion, but as days turned into months, reality set in. Life has a way of stripping away illusions, and for Vikram and Poonam, it was no different.

One bright morning, sunlight streamed into their cosy 23rd-floor apartment. Vikram, a dedicated worker, was prepping for another day at the office. Poonam, equally committed to her studies and household chores, surprised him by waking up early to prepare breakfast and a hearty lunch. For the first time since their wedding, Vikram savoured home-cooked food, filling him with warmth and appreciation. He boasted about Poonam's culinary skills to his colleagues, who were just as delighted.

But amidst these joyful moments, an undercurrent of tension began to surface. It was as if a storm was brewing beneath their seemingly calm life.

Vikram's boss, impressed by his dedication, suggested a weekend getaway to Langkawi, an enchanting island off Malaysia's coast. Vikram shared the idea with Poonam, who welcomed it with open arms. They meticulously planned their trip, choosing a unique resort with rooms made from large water pipes, giving them a front-row view of the serene sea.

The Langkawi trip was a breath of fresh air. They explored the island, took thrilling cable car rides, and visited an aqua museum. Vikram felt like the luckiest man alive, watching Poonam's eyes sparkle with wonder. Those days were filled with laughter, love, and adventures that strengthened their bond.

However, returning to their routine marked a new chapter. Days passed uneventfully until a minor disagreement escalated into a heated argument.

One morning, Vikram's phone rang. His mother, excited and anticipating, asked if Poonam would observe the fast for Karwa Chauth, as it was her first since their marriage. This simple question ignited a fiery dispute. Poonam lashed out at Vikram, questioning why his mother was imposing such traditions when she had clearly expressed her disdain for these rituals before their marriage. The call ended abruptly, leaving Vikram bewildered.

Vikram tried to explain his mother's perspective, emphasising the festival's significance for her. But his words fell on deaf ears. Poonam continued her tirade, criticising Vikram and his family for being conservative and oppressive. Defeated and confused, Vikram left for the office. He had never encountered such a volatile reaction from Poonam. He tried calling her several times during the day to clear the air, but she didn't answer. He found solace in conversations with female colleagues, who excitedly discussed their Karwa Chauth preparations.

After work, Vikram stopped by a bakery to buy Poonam's favourite cake, determined to salvage the evening. He returned home to find Poonam, adorned in a vibrant red saree and jewellery, her face flushed with anger, declaring she would observe the fast—not out of devotion, but in response to what she perceived as pressure from Vikram's family. She hadn't eaten all day, her anger fuelling her resolve

The doorbell rang. His Indian colleague and his wife were at the door. Poonam's demeanour remained pleasant during the visit, and Vikram was grateful for the respite from their recent discord. However, the tension had not dissipated. After their guests departed, Poonam reverted to her cold and distant self, creating an uncomfortable atmosphere at home. The silence between them grew thicker with each passing day.

Weeks passed, and Poonam continued to stonewall Vikram, creating palpable tension. At work, Vikram faced a disappointment that deeply affected him. His boss, who had promised perks and recognition for his relentless efforts, failed to deliver. Vikram contemplated quitting his job, a decision that held immense weight for his career and life in Singapore.

When he shared his dilemma with Poonam, she surprised him by agreeing to leave Singapore and return to India. Her reasons were a mix of boredom and disapproval of Vikram's workplace, leaving him wondering about the true source of her frustrations.

One evening, as they sat amidst half-packed boxes, Poonam finally opened up. Tears streamed down her face as she confessed to feeling isolated and homesick. The city that had once seemed so full of promise now felt like a gilded cage. She missed the familiarity of home, the comfort of her family, and the sense of belonging that Singapore could never provide. Vikram listened, his heart aching at her vulnerability. He realised that he had been so consumed with his own struggles that he had failed to see hers.

They talked late into the night, sharing their fears and doubts. It was the first honest conversation they had had in weeks, and it felt like a weight had been lifted. They both agreed that returning to India might be the fresh start they needed—not as a retreat, but as a strategic move to rebuild their lives and their relationship on firmer ground.

The following days saw Vikram and Poonam preparing to uproot their lives in Singapore with a renewed sense of purpose. Yet, beneath the surface, Vikram couldn't shake the feeling that their relationship was at a crossroads. The path ahead was uncertain, and the once-solid foundation of their love was showing cracks. As they packed their belongings, the weight of the decision hung heavily. Would returning to India bring them happiness, or unveil more challenges? Only time would reveal the answer as Vikram and Poonam embarked on their next chapter, hand in hand, yet with doubts lingering in their hearts.

Chapter Eight

FRACTURED VOWS: A JOURNEY THROUGH TURBULENT SKIES

"Love takes flight, but can it weather the turbulence of life?"

It was nearly midnight when their flight touched down at Indira Gandhi International Airport. November had brought winter's chill to the north, biting at Poonam as she fished out a shawl from her handbag. Vikram, with half his mind on the taxi, half on everything else, finally got them to his sister's place. The surprise wasn't that his sister and brother-in-law were still awake—it was the instant warmth, the kind you feel when you've just finished a long journey and someone's waiting with dinner. Over the meal, they chatted about their upcoming trip to Vikram's native village for post-wedding rituals. His parents were already there, holding down the fort.

The drive to his village was a six-hour marathon, and by the time they arrived, afternoon had already settled in. Vikram's mother greeted them with a feast—something that felt like home in every bite. Poonam, though, was quietly battling her unease during the rituals. She kept her cool, but her emotions were simmering just beneath the surface.

The next few days were a blur of rituals and a grand feast organised by Vikram's parents. As the village festivities wound down, the couple moved on to Patiala for Diwali—Poonam's first as a married woman. She threw herself into decorating the house with flowers, surprising Vikram with a flair he hadn't seen before. During the evening pooja, Vikram's father handed her a pair of gold earrings, and Vikram got the obligatory Diwali cash. The night ended with a feast that left everyone too full to argue about anything.

Vikram's plan after Diwali was simple: drop Poonam off in Pune and head to Bangalore for job hunting. But, like most plans, it didn't survive contact with reality. A random search on a job portal landed him an interview that same evening—and by the end of the day, Vikram had a job offer in hand. When he called Poonam to share the news, her excitement was almost infectious. "Wow, that's awesome! Let's celebrate tonight," she said, making it sound like they had just won the lottery.

Vikram's new job was set to start the following week, and in the meantime, they plotted out Poonam's next steps. He suggested she get a certification that could fast-track her career, which led her to land a role as a junior financial analyst. Their future seemed to be finally slotting into place. They even moved closer to Poonam's office, into a cosy 1 BHK apartment that had all the modern amenities and a garden that was perfect for romantic evening walks. They loved their new place, and for a while, it felt like everything was finally going their way.

But life, as it tends to, threw a curveball. One evening, while they were taking that post-dinner walk in the garden, Vikram's phone rang. His mother was calling—a rare occurrence during the week. Poonam shot him a look that could freeze water, but he picked up anyway. The call turned out to be about his sister's promotion, and it dragged on for 30 minutes. By the time he got off the phone, Poonam had already retreated to bed.

Vikram walked into their room only to be met with an icy silence. "What's wrong?" he asked, hoping it was something he could fix with a few words. But Poonam's anger was a slow boil. "Next time you decide to have a chat with your parents, don't drag me along for a 'leisurely' walk. Got it?" she snapped, her voice dripping with sarcasm.

And just like that, the first crack appeared. They ended up sleeping in separate rooms that night, and it wasn't long before these little spats became a pattern. Vikram made what should have been a minor mistake— booking his parents' flight to Pune without running it by Poonam first. It didn't disrupt her schedule, but she made sure he knew that it should have been a joint decision.

While their personal life started to get messy, Vikram's professional life was on an upswing. He got involved in a new programme at work, and his boss—who pretended to be his biggest supporter—nominated him, fully expecting him to fail. But Vikram's relentless work ethic won out, and he ended up with senior management's approval. His success only deepened his boss's resentment.

Then came an opportunity that could have changed everything – a project in the UK and Austria. Vikram was thrilled, but his boss had already begun undermining him behind the scenes. Though he pretended to be happy for Vikram, he was playing politics, aiming to take the spot himself. When he couldn't, he threw Vikram a bone – a trip to the US. It wasn't what Vikram had hoped for, but he accepted it, albeit reluctantly.

When Vikram told Poonam about the trip, she was supportive and suggested celebrating. They decided on a quiet dinner at the Radisson. Over a meal in an almost-empty restaurant, they talked about the upcoming months. Poonam suggested they vacate their apartment and stay with her mother to save on rent while Vikram was away. It made sense, and Vikram was all for it.

Time flew by, and soon, Vikram was off to the US. Poonam didn't come with him to Mumbai for the send-off, which stung him a bit, but he let it slide. Once he was in San Francisco, everything felt different—the cold, the short days, the lack of warmth in the office where no one seemed to care he was the new guy. The time difference with India meant his calls with Poonam were short and strained. Then, out of nowhere, she hit him with, "Why didn't you insist I join you in the US?" It was like she had been storing up all her frustrations just to blindside him. Their arguments grew more frequent, and the silences in between grew longer.

Vikram tried to focus on work, but the constant fighting was taking its toll. Then, during one particularly bad argument, they decided to call it quits. The decision hung heavy, and a week of silence followed. Finally, Vikram reached out to discuss his return plan to Pune. Her response was cold and distant. He didn't push it, though—he was tired of fighting.

By the time he landed back in Mumbai, Vikram was looking for any sign that things might turn around. But there was no message from Poonam. The drive to Pune felt like a journey to an uncertain future. When he finally arrived, Poonam's mother greeted him with the kind of tired warmth you give to someone you didn't expect to see. "Don't wake her," she said, almost apologetically. Vikram chuckled to himself, realising he should have stopped for breakfast.

When Poonam finally emerged, she was distant, almost as if they were strangers. The next week was a confusing mix of warmth and cold shoulders. Finally, Vikram couldn't take it anymore. "Do you want to end this?" he asked, not sure if he wanted to hear the answer.

Chapter Nine

A Double Blow

"Navigating the Twists and Turns of Life's Journey"

In the bustling city of Pune, where dreams often take shape and love stories find their beginnings, Vikram's life was about to take an unexpected nosedive. The skies above the city seemed overcast with uncertainty, mirroring the storm raging within him. As the days passed, Vikram's once-loving relationship with Poonam morphed into something unrecognisable. The very person who used to light up his world had become a mystery, shrouding herself in a cold and distant demeanour. Their conversations were punctuated with awkward silences, and her responses had become terse and detached.

One fateful evening, after yet another strained conversation, Vikram made a decision that would alter the course of his life. He decided to call it quits. Little did he know this decision would trigger a cascade of events he could never have imagined. Packing his bags in a daze, Vikram booked a place to stay on Airbnb. He hoped that leaving Poonam's place would bring clarity, but he was met with indifference from her parents. Her dad was glued to the news on TV, and her mom was preoccupied in the kitchen. It was as if they had already accepted the impending separation.

Leaving their home, Vikram glanced back at Poonam's parents, searching for a glimmer of understanding or compassion. There was none. He booked a cab, his heart heavy with the realisation that he was truly alone in this city he had come to call home. During the cab ride, Vikram called his dad and shared the heart-wrenching story of what had transpired. His dad, no stranger to Poonam's distant behaviour, did his best to console his son. They talked at length about the recent developments, and Vikram's mom chimed in, worried about how her son would manage without his family nearby.

Throughout the night, Vikram's tears flowed freely as he tried to make sense of it all. He replayed every moment of their relationship in his mind, searching for answers. He had been nothing but supportive, treating Poonam's parents as his own and bending over backwards to fulfil her every wish. Yet, he felt like an outsider in their lives.

Morning came, and Vikram awoke to the shrill sound of his alarm. He felt dizzy and emotionally drained, but the thought of spending the day at the office seemed better than being alone with his thoughts. He pushed himself out of bed, hoping that the routine of work would provide a temporary escape.

In the office, however, Vikram found it impossible to concentrate. His mind wandered during meetings, fixated on the events of the past day. He had once envisioned this year as a time of success and opportunity, with a business trip to the US on the horizon. Now, his life had taken a dark and unexpected turn. As the day wore on, Vikram's ability to focus dwindled further. He decided to take a leave of absence on medical grounds and made plans to visit his parents in Delhi. His flight was booked for the next morning, but before leaving, he felt compelled to visit Poonam's house one last time, despite his family's objections.

Inside Poonam's home, an uneasy hush settled over the living room, casting a palpable tension as family members exchanged uncertain glances. After a pregnant pause, Poonam's mother dispersed the silence by extending a simple offer of water. Vikram nodded appreciatively, accepting the glass, and after a tense beat, he mustered the courage to break the ice.

"How are you, Poonam?" he asked, his voice carrying a delicate blend of hope and despair.

Poonam, still engrossed in her phone, replied brusquely, "Yeah, I am fine."

The response stung, but Vikram swallowed his pride and forged ahead. "I am heading to Delhi tomorrow and will be working from there for a few days."

Poonam's rejoinder dripped with sarcasm, "Oh, that's great. Enjoy your time with your family. But why tell me? I think we've both made a decision."

Vikram's heart sank, yet he endeavoured to diffuse the mounting tension. "I believe we're still together until we officially part ways."

Poonam's mother intervened abruptly, her tone laden with a mix of empathy and finality. "No, we believe it's time to end this. Poonam has shared everything with us, and we genuinely think it's in the best interest of both of you to part ways."

Vikram, grappling with a myriad of emotions, nodded silently. The gravity of the moment hung heavy in the air, as the reality of their impending separation took root in the room. Despite the challenging circumstances, Vikram found himself searching for a glimmer of understanding in Poonam's eyes, hoping against hope for a different outcome.

Vikram couldn't believe his ears. He had hoped that the parents' intervention would lead to reconciliation, but it seemed even they didn't want the relationship to continue. The weight of their words crushed him, making it difficult to breathe. With teary eyes, he left the place, his heart heavy with sorrow.

The next morning, Vikram returned to his childhood home in Delhi, where his mom had prepared his favourite breakfast to lift his spirits. As he quietly ate, his parents waited for him to share his thoughts and feelings, but Vikram remained silent, lost in the turmoil of his emotions. After breakfast, Vikram's dad suggested they go for a walk, hoping to provide a safe space for his son to open up. As they strolled through the neighbourhood, Vikram's dad broached the subject that weighed heavily on both their minds.

"So, what have you decided?" he asked, his voice filled with concern.

Vikram, still lost in thought, suddenly snapped back to the present moment. With a heavy sigh, he replied, "No idea, Dad. I am clueless. But I wish we could stay together. I will try to convince her once again."

Vikram's dad listened patiently as his son poured out his heart, recounting the trials and tribulations of his relationship with Poonam. After a 30-minute monologue, Vikram fell silent, his emotions spent. With a deep, understanding tone, Vikram's dad began to speak, "I understand, Vikram, what you are going through. But you have to be strong. I don't think she wants to stay with you, and neither do her parents. After you left the house, I also talked to them, but they were least interested in discussing it. So, if you ask me, I suggest that you forget her and focus on other things. It will take time, but I think it's the best course of action for you now."

Vikram listened to his father's advice, his heart torn between acceptance and the lingering hope of reconciliation. The streetlamps cast a gentle glow on their faces as Vikram's dad continued, "I know it's tough, son. Relationships are like delicate glass – once shattered, the pieces may never fit perfectly again. But life has a way of offering new beginnings when we least expect it."

He paused, placing a reassuring hand on Vikram's shoulder. "You are young, Vikram. There's a whole world out there waiting for you to explore. Sometimes, letting go is the first step towards finding something even more beautiful."

Vikram took a moment to absorb his father's words, the weight of the situation slowly sinking in. "Dad," he began, his voice trembling, "I just thought we could fix things. I didn't expect it to end like this."

Vikram's dad smiled, a mixture of empathy and wisdom in his eyes. "Life seldom unfolds the way we plan, son. But remember, you are not alone. We will get through this together, one step at a time."

As they continued their walk, the night air became a silent witness to the unspoken bond between father and son, navigating the complexities of love and loss.

After spending a few days with his family, Vikram began to feel a semblance of normalcy returning to his life. He decided to move back to Pune, but his biggest challenge was finding a place to stay, as he had left some of his belongings at Poonam's house. He enlisted the help of a broker to find temporary accommodation while he awaited the completion of his own flat.

Life in Pune became a daily struggle for Vikram. His personal life was in shambles, and his professional life wasn't faring much better. He had been eagerly anticipating a long-term opportunity to relocate to the UK, only to have his hopes dashed by his boss, who assigned him a challenging project with a demanding

Indian client. His dreams of international success were put on hold as he reluctantly accepted the assignment.

Despite the difficulties, Vikram managed to find moments in his hectic day to exchange messages with Poonam. Her responses, however, were consistently cold and harsh. She portrayed herself as the victim and placed blame on Vikram for their deteriorating relationship. Despite the emotional turmoil, Vikram continued to hold out hope that they might reconcile one day.

He tried to find solace in his work, but his frustration and anger soon reached a boiling point. One evening, after a particularly gruelling day at the office, Vikram sat in his dimly lit room, a heavy sense of despair settling over him. It was as if the walls were closing in, suffocating him under the weight of his own thoughts.

As he stared at the ceiling, the realisation hit him like a tidal wave: he couldn't keep living like this. He couldn't keep clinging to the past, hoping for a future that might never come. Vikram knew that if he wanted to find peace, he had to let go. He had to accept that the life he had envisioned with Poonam was not meant to be.

With a trembling hand, Vikram reached for his phone. He scrolled through the messages they had exchanged, reading over the hurtful words that had been exchanged in the heat of the moment. It was painful, but it was also a stark reminder of how far they had drifted apart.

Taking a deep breath, Vikram began to compose a final message. He poured out his heart, expressing his feelings one last time, but also acknowledging that it was time to move on. As he hit send, a sense of closure washed over him. It wasn't the ending he had hoped for, but it was the ending he needed.

In the days that followed, Vikram focused on rebuilding his life. He threw himself into his work, finding solace in the challenges that came with his new project. Slowly but surely, he began to heal, finding strength in the knowledge that he had the power to shape his own future.

Chapter Ten

BROKEN DREAMS: A JOURNEY THROUGH HEARTACHE AND HEALING

"When love shatters, the journey to healing begins."

Vikram woke up to the cold light of dawn, but it felt like he was still trapped in a never-ending nightmare. He lay in his empty bed, the warmth of Poonam's presence a distant, cruel joke. The weight of reality was like a damn lead blanket pressing down on him. For weeks, he'd sensed something was off in their relationship. Yet, he never truly believed it would end. In his mind, Poonam loved him too much to leave—after all, their bond was supposed to be unbreakable, right?

But here's the brutal truth: life doesn't give a damn about what you think should happen. Vikram kept telling himself that Poonam would come back, that they were meant to be the "perfect couple" again. He clung to that hope like a life raft in a stormy sea, even as the waves of reality crashed over him.

Vikram felt a heaviness in his chest, a gnawing doubt that just wouldn't go away. He couldn't face the world today, let alone go to the office. With a heavy sigh, he sent an email to his boss and colleagues, fabricating a sick leave excuse. He stared at his phone, hoping it would ring with Poonam's name. Hours dragged on in the evening, but her call never came. At 8:00 PM, Vikram's patience wore thin. He dialled Poonam's number, heart pounding with the desperate hope of resolving their argument from the night before.

But it wasn't Poonam who answered. It was her mother. Vikram's voice trembled as he recounted their argument, pleading for her help. The reply he got was a punch in the gut. Poonam's mother sided with her decision and told Vikram to move on. The blow was a sucker punch he hadn't seen coming. Baffled and shattered, Vikram felt like he was drowning in an ocean of despair. He needed fresh air, clarity, anything to escape the suffocating weight of his emotions. He stumbled onto the terrace, seeking a distant corner to sit in and stare into the void.

"Why the hell is life so unfair?" he muttered, his voice barely a whisper. He'd always been the one lifting the others up, yet here he was, trapped in his own miserable pit. Negative thoughts consumed him, and he felt darkness closing in. As he gazed over the ledge, a sinister thought crept into his mind—what if he could end all this suffering with a single leap? It flickered like a dangerous beacon, and for a moment, his heart was drawn to its grim promise of escape. He edged closer to the edge, the abyss below calling out to him.

But then, a surge of fear jolted him back. This wasn't who he was. He retreated, engaging in a fierce internal battle. He remembered all the pep talk he'd given to friends, urging them to keep fighting. The irony wasn't lost on him: giving advice was easy, living it was the hard part. Amidst the turmoil, a glimmer of hope sparked. He thanked whatever force had stopped him from making a tragic mistake. Muttering Rocky's famous line, he found a semblance of strength in the idea that life wasn't about how hard you hit, but how hard you could keep moving forward. He decided to face his troubles head-on, no matter how daunting they seemed.

The next morning, Vikram called his father, his voice tinged with uncertainty as he recounted the mess with Poonam. His father, ever the pillar of support, listened with patience. He offered reassurance, suggesting that something better might be waiting for Vikram in the future. The unwavering support of his family gave him a glimmer of hope.

Determined to tackle his situation, Vikram turned to Google, seeking ways to cope with a breakup. He dove into articles and blogs from people who had survived similar pain. Divorce, he learned, was a unique journey, a tangled web of emotions. Armed with this newfound knowledge, Vikram crafted his survival strategy. No drowning sorrows in alcohol or fixating on memories. Instead, he immersed himself in self-help books, their words of encouragement becoming his lifeline. He embraced self-care routines, connected with friends, adopted healthy habits, and explored new horizons.

He began integrating these suggestions into his daily routine, finding solace in the small victories amidst the darkness.

Despite his efforts, the separation was gut-wrenching. The decision to end their relationship wasn't his, and he struggled with feelings of rejection and insecurity. He had loved Poonam deeply, and her absence left an enormous void. The strength of their bond had seemed unshakeable, and the thought of it crumbling so easily was almost impossible to accept.

Desperate to salvage something, Vikram suggested couples therapy, hoping it could mend the rift. Poonam, however, was firm. She blamed him for their issues and insisted he seek therapy on his own. With no other options, Vikram agreed and searched for therapists. He found a range of options, from clinical psychologists to psychiatrists. Uncertain about the differences, he did some research and eventually booked an appointment with a clinical psychologist, hoping this session would offer the clarity he desperately needed.

As he lay on his bed, contemplating his uncertain future, his phone rang. It was his father. Vikram answered with a mix of apprehension and relief.

"Hey, Dad," Vikram greeted, attempting to sound composed.

"We're good," his father replied warmly. "How are you doing? Did you have dinner?"

"Yeah," Vikram said. "I ordered from Zomato. It should be here soon. What about you?"

When Vikram mentioned his upcoming therapy appointment, his father's concern was palpable.

"Why counselling? You don't need a therapist. Panditji has remedies. Your mother's already handling that. No need for counselling."

Vikram tried to explain, "Dad, it's just a way for me to gain clarity. I want to make sure I am making the right decisions."

His father, still unsure, finally relented. "Do as you wish. We are with you, no matter what. But remember, we have always shared everything. Why not talk to us instead of a stranger?"

Vikram sighed. "I know, Dad. It's just that sometimes an outsider can offer a fresh perspective."

His father nodded thoughtfully. "Alright, if you think it will help. But remember, we're here for you, always."

Vikram hung up, his father's disapproval still hanging in the air. He knew he had to forge his own path, no matter how uncertain it seemed. The next evening, as he headed to the therapist's office, Vikram left behind a world of shattered dreams and stepped into one filled with uncertainty and hope. He was ready to find the answers he sought, no matter where the journey took him.

Chapter Eleven

FROM HEARTACHE TO HOPE

"When love shatters, the journey to rebuild a
resilient heart begins."

In the brightly lit clinic, where motivational posters clung to the walls like desperate promises, Vikram approached the receptionist. She was annoyingly cheerful, the kind of person who probably believed in affirmations and green smoothies.

"Yes, sir," she beamed. "You have an appointment at 5 PM. Dr. Denaz will be here in another 10 minutes. Please wait there," she pointed to a couch that screamed 'therapy session'.

Vikram plopped onto the couch, his mind swirling with the kind of thoughts that gnaw at you when you're facing a life unravelling at the seams. People hurried in and out of the doctor's room, like they had somewhere better to be. It was 5:10 PM when the receptionist finally nodded at him. "You can go in now."

He knocked on the door, and a voice, warm yet authoritative, invited him in. Dr. Denaz, with her calm presence and a smile that seemed to know too much, greeted him. Vikram felt a strange mix of comfort and dread.

"Hello, Madam," he began, his voice wavering. "I am in the middle of a separation. We're talking about a mutual consent divorce, but I am not sure if this is what I want. I suggested marriage counselling, but my wife shut it down. I am here to figure out what went wrong and if there's anything left to save."

Dr. Denaz listened, her silence almost unnerving as Vikram poured out years of frustration, guilt, and confusion. After what felt like a lifetime of unloading, he finally sighed, "I think she's egotistic."

The doctor put her notebook aside and looked him straight in the eye. "No, Vikram. She's not egoistic. What you're describing sounds more like emotional unavailability."

Vikram's eyebrows shot up. "Emotionally unavailable? What does that even mean?"

"Emotionally immature people," she began, "see the world in black and white. They're terrified of ambiguity, hate taking risks, and can't stand admitting they're wrong. They are like emotional toddlers—stubborn, self-centred, and exhausting."

Vikram nodded, feeling the sting of truth in her words. She continued, "These people need constant attention but avoid anything that makes them vulnerable. They might even act out, changing the subject, withdrawing, or getting aggressive just to avoid feeling anything too deeply."

"It's like you have just described the last five years of my life," Vikram said, a bitter chuckle escaping his lips. "But what do I do? Can this be fixed?"

Dr. Denaz's expression softened. "Relationships are messy, Vikram, especially when one person refuses to fully commit. You can't fix what she won't admit is broken."

He sighed, a heavy sound that carried the weight of his fading hope. "I have tried talking to her. She just blames me for everything and refuses to even consider help."

"She's stuck in a victim complex," Dr. Denaz said, leaning forward. "And here's the hard truth: people like this can change, but only if they want to. You can't force someone to grow up. They have to decide to do that themselves."

Vikram stared at the floor, his determination faltering. "So, what do I do?"

"You have already taken a big step by seeking help," she said. "But ask yourself, can you keep living like this? Can you handle more of the same, day after day, year after year? If you have done all you can, maybe it's time to let go."

His heart twisted at the thought, but he knew she was right. "Thank you, Doctor. This gives me a lot to think about."

As Vikram left the clinic, the conversation replayed in his head, a mix of relief and sorrow settling in his chest. The doctor's words were a balm, but also a challenge. Could he really walk away from a life he'd spent years building?

That night, alone in his dimly lit room, Vikram's thoughts spiralled. The options Dr. Denaz had laid out felt impossible to navigate. The silence was broken by his phone ringing. It was Poonam.

"Hey, Vikram. Is this a good time?" Her voice was casual, almost too casual for what they were about to discuss.

"Yeah, we can talk," he replied, though he wasn't sure he wanted to.

"So, I talked to a lawyer. She says a mutual consent divorce would save us money. What do you think? Should we just get this over with, or do you want to drag it out with another lawyer?"

Her words hit him like a slap. "Can we at least try marriage counselling?" he asked, desperation creeping into his tone.

"No," she said, her voice as cold as the decision she had made long ago. "We have tried. It's over. Let's just move on."

Vikram's chest tightened. "Okay, let's proceed with the divorce. Just tell me what you need."

The call ended, and Vikram was left in the silence of his own making. He hadn't wanted this, but it was happening, and there was nothing he could do to stop it.

The next morning, an email from the lawyer landed in his inbox. By evening, the affidavit was ready. Everything was moving too fast, too efficiently, like a machine designed to dismantle his life. The first hearing was scheduled for Saturday.

When the day arrived, Vikram found himself at the lawyer's office, where Poonam waited with her friends, laughing and showing off pictures like it was just another day. Vikram stayed silent, feeling the sting of her detachment. After signing the papers, they headed to court, where the judge set the final hearing six months out.

The reality of his choice hit him hard as he returned home. The life he knew was slipping away, and he was powerless to stop it.

Searching the internet for answers only deepened his confusion. Advice ranged from venting on social media to finding comfort in friends or therapy. But one piece of wisdom stood out, echoing something his father used to say: "When life hits you hard, you have two options—be better or be bitter."

Vikram chose to be better. He decided to turn this painful chapter into one of growth, resilience, and self-discovery. And so, with a heavy heart but a clear mind, he set out on a path to rebuild his life, one step at a time.

Chapter Twelve

THE CALL OF ADVENTURE

"Answering Life's Challenges with Courage"

Vikram had always been a planner, a meticulous architect of his life. So when the idea of a solo journey popped into his head, it wasn't a spur-of-the-moment decision. He spent hours scouring the internet, his mind oscillating between the need to escape and the fear of the unknown. Eventually, he stumbled upon Spiti—a rugged, unforgiving corner of India that seemed like the perfect place to outrun his inner demons. Without a second thought, he booked a road trip to the Spiti Valley, his heart whispering that this was his ticket to a fresh start.

As the departure day loomed, Vikram's anticipation was palpable. He prepped for the journey as if it were a matter of life and death, obsessing over every detail. But life had other plans. Just two days before he was set to leave, his phone buzzed, the tour operator's number flashing on the screen like a bad omen.

"Hello, sir," the voice on the other end was almost too polite, a harbinger of bad news.

Vikram's heart sank. He wasn't sure why, but he had a hunch this wasn't a routine confirmation call. "I'm good," he replied, masking his concern.

"Sir, I regret to inform you that due to unforeseen circumstances, we must cancel your Spiti trip. However, we can accommodate you on a confirmed trip to Kedar Kantha next week."

In an instant, Vikram's excitement evaporated, replaced by a surge of frustration. He had meticulously planned this trip, arranged his leave, shopped for gear—and now, this. The operator's calm explanation about adverse weather did little to soothe him. He felt like he was being robbed of his escape.

"Fine," he snapped, anger masking the creeping sense of helplessness. "What's this Kedar Kantha trek?"

As he Googled the trek, his initial irritation gave way to doubt. The images were breathtaking, but a five-day trek through unforgiving terrain. He wasn't in the shape for this. Hell, he wasn't in the shape for anything, physically or emotionally. But maybe that's exactly why he needed to go. Reluctantly, he agreed, knowing deep down that this might be the jolt his life needed.

The night before the trek, Vikram arrived at the meeting point, his nervous energy barely concealed beneath a forced smile. The group was a mixed bag—two lively girls from Mumbai, three middle-aged ladies from Bangalore, a couple from Chandigarh, and a trio of young men brimming with a reckless energy that made Vikram feel old and weary. He quickly dubbed them the "Three Musketeers."

As they embarked on the journey to the base camp, Vikram's mind was a whirlpool of doubts. Could he really do this? Was this just another bad decision in a long line of them? That night, as they gathered around the dinner table, one of the Musketeers noticed his unease.

"What's on your mind, Vikram, sir? You seem tense," the guy asked, his tone casual but concerned.

Vikram hesitated, then decided to be honest. "I'm not sure I'm cut out for this trek. I haven't been active in years, and honestly, I'm just not sure I can do it."

The Musketeer didn't miss a beat. "Don't worry, Vikram, sir. We've got your back. We will drag you to the top if we have to."

For the first time in days, Vikram laughed—a real, unforced laugh. "Thanks, man. Let's do this together."

The next few days were a blur of exhaustion, camaraderie, and more self-doubt than Vikram cared to admit. The trek was brutal—biting cold, high-speed winds, and terrain that tested every ounce of his willpower. But the Three Musketeers kept their promise. They were relentless in their support, lifting his spirits when the weight of his thoughts threatened to pull him under.

Standing at the summit, Vikram was overwhelmed by the panoramic view of the Himalayas, the morning sun casting a divine glow on the pristine snow. The freezing winds bit at his skin, but inside, he felt a warmth he hadn't known in years. The climb had broken something open in him, something that had been locked away since his marriage fell apart. He realised then that it wasn't just about reaching the top; it was about rediscovering a part of himself he thought he'd lost—a part that was stronger, braver, and capable of overcoming anything.

The next few weeks were a blur of highs and lows. The trek had given him a taste of what life could be like without the constant emotional baggage he'd been dragging around. But just as he started to enjoy the newfound freedom, the familiar ache of longing returned. He found himself missing Poonam, despite everything she'd put him through. It was like a part of him was still stuck in the past, hoping for a miracle that would never come.

One evening, as the loneliness became too much to bear, Vikram decided to open up to his family. He hoped that sharing his feelings might offer some clarity. But, as expected, their well-meaning advice fell flat.

"Vikram, it's normal to feel this way after a five-year relationship. But you need to stay strong and not forget how she treated you. This is just a passing phase."

Their words were meant to comfort, but they left Vikram feeling more isolated than ever. He realised he needed professional help to navigate the emotional labyrinth he was trapped in. Without overthinking it, he booked an appointment with Dr. Denaz.

The day of the appointment arrived, and Vikram found himself in the waiting room, his nerves jangling like a live wire. When Dr. Denaz finally called him in, her warm smile and gentle demeanour instantly put him at ease.

"Hi Vikram, how are you?" she asked, her tone friendly but professional. "And how are things with your spouse?"

"We've applied for a mutual consent divorce," Vikram replied, trying to sound detached. "We are in the cooling-off period."

"That's good to hear. Acceptance is the first step," she said, nodding. "So, what brings you here today?"

Vikram took a deep breath and began to unload. He talked about the strange mix of emotions that plagued him—how he knew divorce was the right decision but couldn't shake the feeling of loss, of something unfinished. Dr. Denaz listened patiently, then dropped a bombshell that shook him to his core.

"Vikram, what you're experiencing is called trauma bonding,"

"Trauma bonding?" he repeated, the term sounding foreign yet disturbingly familiar.

"It's when you form a deep emotional attachment to someone who harms you," she explained. "It's common in abusive relationships, where periods of mistreatment are interspersed with moments of affection. It creates a cycle that's incredibly hard to break."

As she spoke, Vikram felt a knot in his stomach. Everything she said hit home. The constant push-pull, the way he still missed Poonam despite everything—it all started to make sense.

"You still miss her because you're emotionally attached, despite the abuse," Dr. Denaz continued. "This kind of attachment is hard to break on your own, but acknowledging it is the first step."

Vikram felt a mixture of relief and dread. On one hand, it was a relief to finally understand why he felt so stuck. On the other hand, the road to recovery seemed daunting.

"What should I do?" he asked, feeling more vulnerable than he had in years.

"We will work on weakening this bond," Dr. Denaz said. "We will explore the patterns of abuse, establish boundaries, and develop a self-care plan. It won't be easy, but you're already on the right path."

Vikram nodded, grateful for her guidance. He knew it wasn't going to be a quick fix, but for the first time in a long time, he felt hopeful.

As he left the clinic, a strange feeling washed over him—something between relief and resolve. Understanding the nature of his emotional attachment to Poonam was like finding a key to a door he didn't know existed. It wouldn't be easy, but he was ready to walk through it, one step at a time. And just like that, the journey of healing began—not with a bang, but with a quiet, determined resolve to reclaim his life.

Chapter Thirteen

THE TRANSFORMATION BEGINS

"Awakening the Inner Journey"

As Vikram sat in his small, cosy apartment that Saturday evening, he couldn't help but feel a mix of relief and scepticism. The words of Dr. Denaz had hit him hard, no doubt, but he wondered if this newfound determination was just another phase—like those gym memberships that start with enthusiasm and end with excuses. Still, something inside him refused to let this moment slip away.

He opened his laptop, grabbed a notebook, and started listing things he wanted to pursue. For too long, his dreams and desires had been buried beneath the wreckage of his failed marriage, suffocated by the weight of disappointment. First on the list: playing the guitar. It was a long-held dream from his college days, a dream he'd always put off because life—marriage, work, and the relentless pursuit of "being an adult"—got in the way. Now, with nothing left to lose, he figured, why the hell not? He quickly searched for guitar classes nearby and found one just a short drive away. Without a second thought, he enrolled for the next available session. No more procrastination, no more waiting for the "right time."

Next up was tennis. Vikram had always admired the elegance and power of tennis players, but the thought of actually getting on a court himself had always felt a little ridiculous. Still, the idea of learning something new excited him—maybe it was the challenge, or maybe it was the hope that chasing down tennis balls might help him outrun his own thoughts. He signed up for a beginners' class at a local sports club, his heart pounding with a mix of excitement and dread. He'd probably suck at first, but at least he'd be moving.

Yoga was another item on his list. It wasn't just the physical benefits he was after; he craved the peace of mind that seemed to elude him lately. The chaos in his head needed a break, and yoga promised just that. A quick online search led him to a nearby studio, and he scheduled his first session. Maybe this was the tranquillity he'd been chasing all along.

But it wasn't just about picking up new hobbies. Vikram knew deep down that he needed to become a fitter, healthier version of himself—not just physically, but mentally and emotionally too. It was about reclaiming his life, one small victory at a time. So, he hired a personal trainer at his apartment's gym. This wasn't just about burning calories; it was about proving to himself that he was worth the effort.

The days that followed were a whirlwind of activity and emotion. The guitar classes were tougher than he'd expected, but with each new chord, he felt a tiny spark of joy—something he hadn't felt in a long time. The music filled his apartment, pushing out the silence that had once felt so suffocating. Tennis, on the other hand, was both humbling and exhilarating. He wasn't great at it, not yet, but the physical exertion felt good—like he was sweating out the poison of his past.

Yoga became his sanctuary. In the studio's calm, he found a space where he could let go, even if just for an hour. Dr. Denaz's words about self-compassion started to make more sense as he let himself be imperfect, messy, and human.

But it wasn't all smooth sailing. Some days, Vikram felt like a fraud—like he was pretending to be this "new and improved" version of himself, while the old wounds were just waiting to resurface. Yet, every time those doubts crept in, he reminded himself that change wasn't supposed to be easy. Growth hurt. It was uncomfortable. And maybe that was okay.

Evenings were no longer dominated by thoughts of Poonam and the life they had failed to build together. Instead, they were filled with the sweet melodies of the guitar, the satisfying thwack of tennis balls, and the quiet serenity of the yoga studio. Vikram was transforming, not just physically, but on a deeper, more profound level.

One evening, as he sat on his yoga mat, ready for another session of deep meditation, a thought struck him like lightning. Dr. Denaz's words about people coming into our lives for a purpose suddenly made sense. Poonam had been a part of his journey, sure, but their paths had diverged for a reason. She had given him lessons—painful, but valuable—and it was time to let go of the resentment that had been eating him alive.

His perspective began to shift. Instead of wallowing in what could have been, Vikram started to focus on what could still be. His journey toward self-love was far from over, but he was finally starting to see the light at the end of the tunnel. His friends and family noticed the change—noticed that he was no longer the ghost of the man he used to be. They saw his energy, his determination, and maybe even a spark of the old Vikram that had been lost for so long.

One night, while strumming his guitar, Vikram received a message from Dr. Denaz. It read, "Vikram, I hope you're doing well on your journey of self-love. Remember, it's a lifelong commitment, but the rewards are immeasurable. Keep thriving!" He couldn't help but smile. He had come a long way from that broken man who had walked out of the doctor's office, lost and defeated. With the guidance of Dr. Denaz, Vikram had found his path to self-discovery, self-love, and maybe, just maybe, a brighter future.

The journey was far from over, but for the first time in a long time, Vikram felt ready to face whatever came next. He wasn't fixed—hell, he wasn't even close—but he was learning to be okay with that. The music filled the room, not as a distraction from his pain, but as a testament to the new life he was slowly but surely creating.

Chapter Fourteen

CRAFTING A BLUEPRINT FOR CHANGE

"Chasing Dreams, One Step at a Time"

Next few weeks were bustling with activity. His days were packed, leaving little room to dwell on his past. Mornings kicked off with tennis, followed by a quick breakfast. Office tasks filled his midday, and evenings were devoted to workouts. Weekends chimed in with guitar classes. All these engagements acted like a shield, momentarily numbing his pain. But just like any quick fix, this relief was fleeting.

Around two weeks in, the energy that once soared began to plummet. Frustration brewed as his routine wore him down. He found himself drained throughout the day, realising he might have taken on more than he could handle. Helplessness crept in, and he questioned whether he could ever break free from this cycle of despair and darkness.

He grabbed his phone, pulled up his favourite spiritual guru's channel, and began searching for tips to escape his current predicament. As he watched a video, something clicked inside him. The guru explained that when we desperately chase our dreams, we often forget that transformation takes time. Just like how things didn't go south in a day, it took a series of missteps, poor decisions, and bad luck to land him in this situation. There were no shortcuts.

The guru's advice was crystal clear: instead of overwhelming himself with too many tasks, he needed to take small, manageable steps. It was like a lightbulb moment for Vikram. He finally knew what he had to do to break free from this situation. He decided to put his management skills to work for a life-changing transformation.

With a notepad in hand, he played some soothing music, creating an atmosphere that sparked deep reflection. As he began, he made a list of the three most important things in his life and then crafted a time-bound plan to achieve them. But what truly caught his attention was the term 'self-care' mentioned by Dr. Denaz. It struck a chord in his mind. He realised that to become a better version of himself, he needed to focus on taking care of his physical, mental, and emotional well-being.

He embarked on a journey of personal transformation. He initiated his transformation with a series of short-term goals and established daily routines aimed at their attainment. In the same way that we trim excess fat from our bodies to enhance our vitality, Vikram resolved to eliminate unproductive habits that served as distractions from his goals.

For his physical well-being, he committed to maintaining his tennis classes, held on alternate days in the early morning, and on the remaining days, he scheduled sessions at his apartment gym. In addition to these activities, he wisely subscribed to a handful of apps that would aid him in tracking his calorie intake, as well as an online yoga and meditation platform to nurture his mental and emotional wellness.

Determined to evolve into the best version of himself, Vikram approached his daily regimen with boundless energy and enthusiasm. He recognised the significance of investing in himself, exemplifying the teachings of renowned transformation and habit coaches like James Clear, author of 'Atomic Habits,' who emphasises the power of small, consistent changes. In sync with Charles Duhigg's 'The Power of Habit,' Vikram understood that by altering his routines and cultivating healthier habits, he was primed for a significant personal transformation.

With an eagerness for progress, Vikram took proactive steps, such as purchasing new athletic shoes and visiting Decathlon to acquire a brand-new tennis racket. However, his very first day back in the tennis class proved to be a humbling experience. The toll that the COVID-19 pandemic and the pressures of both his professional and personal life had taken on his physical fitness became unmistakably evident. He struggled to hit even a few balls and could barely sustain five minutes of continuous play.

Observing Vikram's challenges, his coach wisely suggested he take a brief respite before rejoining the class. At that moment, Vikram had a revelation—a fundamental realisation that his transformation journey, much like those coached by experts such as Tony Robbins or Mel Robbins, would not unfold without its share of obstacles and setbacks. Nevertheless, he remained steadfast in his determination to persevere, knowing that true personal transformation required patience, resilience, and an unwavering commitment to his goals.

As Vikram took a breather in the court corner, he found himself approached by Pramod, a guy in his mid-thirties boasting an athletic build. Vikram observed Pramod's skilled play, his impressive fitness level, and his impeccable techniques that made him look like a seasoned pro.

"Hey there, buddy. You look a bit worn out," Pramod remarked with a grin.

Vikram chuckled, "Yeah, trying to catch my breath. Today's my first day giving tennis a shot, and honestly, I haven't done anything physical in ages. Feels like there's a long road ahead."

Pramod nodded sympathetically, "I did notice you were having a bit of a struggle out there. But hey, don't let that get you down. Taking the leap into tennis is a fantastic first step towards a healthier lifestyle. And you know what, to really boost your progress, keeping an eye on your diet is just as crucial. Eating right is the key."

"Thanks for the advice, Pramod. Your tips mean a lot," Vikram expressed his gratitude. "By the way, I don't think we've officially met. I'm Vikram." He extended his hand towards Pramod.

Pramod warmly shook his hand, "No worries at all, Vikram. I'm Pramod. Apologies for not introducing myself earlier. If you ever need more tips or just want to chat about tennis or anything else, I'm here. Let's make this tennis journey a fun one!"

The coaching session was over. The coach called it a day. All the players greeted each other and headed home.

While taking a shower, Vikram was pondering Pramod's sage advice about adopting a healthier diet. He'd already set his sights on a transformation of his eating habits, and what better moment to commence than now? So, with great determination, he resolved to take the plunge. For his inaugural act of dietary redemption, he boldly opted for Chana bhatura for breakfast, reasoning that one last indulgence wouldn't hurt. He comforted himself with the notion that his journey towards virtuous eating was just around the corner.

With unwavering enthusiasm, he embarked on a quest for healthy eating plans, and to his sheer astonishment, the internet served up a smorgasbord of diet options. Some of these digital fitness gurus, armed with their extraordinary claims, promised everything from shedding pounds faster than you can say "bikini season" to magically vanishing inches from one's waistline in a mere three weeks.

Though Vikram couldn't help but acknowledge that such extravagant assertions were more fiction than fact, he decided to humour them. In a fit of irony, he even subscribed to one such diet plan, generously endorsed by a famous fitness influencer, who apparently possessed the secret to transforming mere mortals into Greek gods in record time.

Armed with a wealth of information, Vikram embarked on his dietary journey. His fitness guru had recommended eliminating all junk food and replacing it with high-protein, high-fibre, and low-carb options for weight reduction. Vikram was initially fuelled by motivation and enthusiasm. He promptly ordered a jar of peanut butter and subscribed to salads from the renowned salad bar in town.

The initial days of his diet journey were remarkable. This new lifestyle was a refreshing change, and Vikram savoured every moment of it. However, this euphoria was short-lived. Just one week into the diet, cravings for his beloved chole bhatura and Thumbs Up soda began to gnaw at him. For a man whose staple diet had been pizza and burgers, successfully abstaining from junk for nearly a week was a monumental achievement.

Yet, after holding out for one more day, Vikram eventually succumbed to the irresistible allure of bhatura and Thumbs Up. As he took the first bite of the fluffy bhatura, he felt as though he had tasted nectar. He devoured it with lightning speed, but immediately after, a heavy blanket of guilt descended upon him. He couldn't help but berate himself for not sticking to his diet plan and questioned his commitment to a healthier lifestyle. He felt disheartened and weak, viewing himself as a failure, wondering if he would ever break free from the clutches of junk food and truly maintain discipline in his diet. However, he wasn't a complete flop. Despite hitting a few bumps on his path to physical fitness and a healthier diet, he was acing the game when it came to his mental and emotional well-being. In this journey of transformation, he took a digital route as well. He subscribed to a meditation app and dove into the world of mindfulness. Unlike his endeavours in tennis and dietary adjustments, he maintained remarkable discipline with his meditation routine. Every morning, without fail, he'd sit down for his meditation session. Soon enough, he began to reap the rewards. His mind became a serene oasis, and he felt more relaxed than ever. This was a silver lining for Vikram; at least he was excelling in one aspect of his transformation journey.

However, deep down, a tiny cloud of dissatisfaction still lingered. The initial setbacks in his transformation journey continued to sting him at the core.

Chapter Fifteen

EMBRACING LIFE'S IMPERFECTIONS

"Resilience in the Face of Setbacks"

It had been a little over a month since Vikram committed to his routine. While he navigated a few bumps along the way, he managed to stay the course—mostly. But today, on the tennis court, he was unravelling. His serves were off, his coach was displeased, and so was he. Frustration simmered under his skin, a slow burn that had been building for weeks. No matter what he tried, he couldn't nail that serve. It was like some cosmic joke, a puzzle he was too damn tired to solve.

Seeing Vikram's growing irritation, the coach advised him to take a break and start afresh. Vikram trudged to a corner, grabbed his water bottle, and took a sip, letting the cool liquid distract him from the storm in his mind.

What the hell was going wrong?

He wondered. Was he even cut out for this? Should he just quit and try something else? The thoughts spiralled, doubts clawing at the edges of his resolve.

Lost in his thoughts, he didn't notice Pramod until the familiar voice cut through the haze.

"Hey there, bro! What's up?" Pramod's smile was infectious, his tone light.

Startled, Vikram turned, a bit embarrassed to be caught off guard. "I'm good, sir. How are you?"

Pramod chuckled. "Cut the 'sir' crap, Vikram. You know I hate that." He paused, catching the tension in Vikram's posture. "You look a bit lost, though. Everything alright?"

Vikram sighed, realising he could let down his guard with Pramod. He spilled out everything—his frustrations, his doubts, the nagging feeling that he was wasting his time.

Pramod listened, genuinely listened, with the kind of patience that's rare these days. When Vikram finally ran out of steam, Pramod suggested they grab coffee at Café Junoon later, offering an escape from the relentless self-critique swirling in Vikram's mind.

At 7:00 p.m., Vikram arrived at Café Junoon. The dim lighting, the mellow live music—it was exactly the kind of place where you could let the world fade away. Spotting Pramod at a corner table, Vikram waved back and joined him.

"Nice place," Vikram remarked as he settled in.

"Yeah, it's where I come to think," Pramod replied. "It's got that vibe, you know? Helps clear the clutter upstairs." He laughed, but there was a truth in his words that Vikram felt in his gut.

They ordered coffee—two mochas, extra chocolate—and Pramod didn't waste time. "So, what's eating at you?"

Vikram took a deep breath. "It's tennis. I've been at it for a month, and I still can't get the hang of serving. Everyone else seems to be improving, but I'm stuck. It's making me wonder if I should just quit and try something else."

Pramod's eyes narrowed slightly. He wasn't just listening—he was diagnosing. "You're in your head too much, man. Look, it's normal to hit a wall. But you've got to stop comparing yourself to others. That's a recipe for misery."

Vikram nodded, but it didn't make the frustration vanish. "I know, but it's hard when you're putting in the effort and not seeing the results."

Pramod leaned back, taking a thoughtful sip of his coffee. "Let me tell you something I learned a while back. Everyone's always in a rush to get somewhere, to achieve something. We're fed this idea that success should be instant. But that's bullshit. The truth is it takes time. Discipline. And yeah, a lot of the time, it feels like you're getting nowhere."

Vikram appreciated the bluntness. It was refreshing to hear someone say it like it was, no sugar-coating. But the words also stung because they hit so close to home.

"Still," Vikram sighed, "it's frustrating as hell. It's like no matter how hard I try, I can't make it work. And that sucks."

Pramod nodded, his gaze steady. "It does. And that's life, man. Unfair, unpredictable, and sometimes downright cruel. But it's also what makes it interesting."

He paused, letting the weight of his words sink in before continuing. "I once met this old beggar on the streets—a guy who'd seen everything and lost it all. He told me something I'll never forget: 'Life isn't about controlling the outcome. It's about embracing the unpredictability and finding your peace within it.'"

Vikram stared at his coffee, reflecting on Pramod's story. It resonated with something deep inside him, something that had been buried under layers of frustration and doubt.

"Maybe that's what I need to do," Vikram said slowly, as if the idea were forming in real time. "Stop trying to control everything and just... go with it."

Pramod smiled. "Exactly. Fix what you can inside, and the outside will follow. But don't rush it. Change doesn't happen overnight."

After their conversation, Vikram felt a strange calm settle over him. He knew he had a long way to go, but the path ahead didn't seem as daunting. He was ready to take it one step at a time, starting with himself.

Back home, Vikram resumed his mindfulness practice, something he'd started a while ago but never fully committed to. Now, it felt like the missing piece. He even joined a yoga class, something that had been on his mind for a while, inspired by the idea of connecting body, mind, and spirit.

As the days turned into weeks, Vikram noticed a change. He was calmer, more focused. The frustration that had once consumed him was now just a background noise, easily tuned out.

And with this new sense of balance, Vikram turned his attention to another area of his life that had been on hold—finding a life partner. He approached it with the same calm determination, crafting his profile on dating sites, not obsessing over the results but focusing on what he could control.

When he started receiving responses, he took it all in his stride. Some connections fizzled out, others ghosted him, and a few showed promise. But he didn't let the setbacks get to him. He knew now that the process was just as important as the outcome.

Finally, after what felt like an eternity of searching, he found someone who clicked with Riya.

She was almost everything he had been looking for, and, more importantly, she was real, grounded in the same realities that Vikram had come to accept.

They talked over the weekend, and as they talked, Vikram realised something. This wasn't just about finding a partner; it was about finding someone who understood the journey he was on. And for the first time in a long time, Vikram felt like he was exactly where he needed to be.

Chapter Sixteen

A New Beginning

"Transformed and ready for love."

Vikram had travelled to Delhi with plans of meeting someone special, only to have those plans collapse at the last minute due to unforeseen circumstances. Rather than wallowing in disappointment, Vikram chose to see it as a serendipitous turn of events. He eagerly called Riya to see if she was free for a coffee. They agreed to meet at the charming United Coffee House. Vikram arrived right on time at 2:00 PM, picked a cosy table, and waited with a mix of anticipation and hope.

Riya, a graceful 35-year-old with a slender frame and a warm wheatish complexion, arrived looking effortlessly stylish. Her calm and confident demeanour was both captivating and genuine. Vikram stood up, pulling out a chair for her with a smile.

"Hello, Vikram," Riya greeted, her voice warm and sincere. "I'm really sorry for making you wait. I felt terrible about it."

Vikram waved it off with a reassuring smile. "No need to apologise. I just got here myself."

With a touch of affection, Vikram asked, "What would you like to have, Riya?".

Riya considered for a moment, her eyes meeting his. "Anything cold would be perfect; it's scorching outside."

Vikram signalled the server and ordered two refreshing mocktails and a delicious margarita pizza. As they waited for their drinks, a comfortable silence settled between them.

Breaking the silence, Vikram leaned in closer. "So, Riya, tell me more about yourself."

And so began a conversation that felt both intimate and effortless. They shared stories from their past, discussed their current lives, and dreamt about their future together. When their food and drinks arrived, their connection remained unbroken, and time seemed to fly. They were so engrossed in each other that they lost track of time until Riya's phone rang. It was a quarter past five, and she had plans to go shopping with her cousins.

With a promise to catch up later, Riya said, "Vikram, I need to go, but let's continue this conversation over the phone."

Back home, Vikram's family eagerly awaited the details of his meeting. His mother had already received glowing feedback from her friend. When Vikram shared his own positive impressions, their excitement was palpable. It was clear that love had made its presence felt that day.

Later, Vikram's phone buzzed with the unmistakable WhatsApp jingle. It was well past his usual bedtime, so he wondered, "Who the heck is messaging me at this hour?" Unlocking his phone, his heart raced – it was Riya!

"Hey Vikram, how's life treating you?" Riya's message appeared, and Vikram couldn't help but grin. "Can we catch up over a call tonight if you're up for it?" she asked.

Vikram had hoped for this but wasn't ready to make the first move. Grateful for the chance, he dialled her number immediately.

Their late-night chats became a cherished routine, a secret rendezvous where they shared their days, exchanged secrets, and dreamt together. Even when Vikram was adventuring in Spiti Valley, Riya was there virtually. He'd send her breathtaking pictures of the valley, and she'd respond with stunning photos from family weddings, looking drop-dead gorgeous. Vikram couldn't help but show them off to his mother, who was already mentally planning their future wedding. They discussed their future with ease, right down to the last detail. Vikram felt on top of the world, imagining a life with Riya.

Then, out of the blue, Riya's messages began to slow, and her responses became less frequent. Confused but not ready to jump to conclusions, Vikram decided to call her.

When Riya answered, she launched into a whirlwind of apologies. "Hey, Vikram, I'm really sorry. Work's been crazy, and I got sick after the wedding. I didn't mean to ghost you."

Vikram listened patiently. "I appreciate you being honest. But I need to know, is everything cool between us? Our recent chats haven't felt the same. What's going on?"

There was a pause before Riya confessed, "Vikram, I've been thinking about us, and it's just not the same anymore. You're an amazing guy, perfect on paper, but the spark seems to have flickered out. I needed some time to process this. I wasn't trying to ghost you."

Vikram, staying true to his calm demeanour, responded, "No worries, Riya. If the connection isn't there, it isn't there. We don't owe anyone anything, and honesty is what matters."

"Thanks for understanding," Riya said, sounding relieved. "We can still be friends, though. Let's catch up when you're back in Delhi."

Vikram, following his heart, replied, "Thanks, Riya, but I'm looking for something more than friendship right now. I wish you all the best. Goodbye." He ended the call, feeling a pang of disappointment but also a surge of pride. He had navigated the situation with grace, thanks to his emotional resilience. Ready to face the world, Vikram remained open to the possibility of love, even if it came with a touch of heartbreak.

With unyielding determination, he set out on a quest to find his soulmate. He registered on numerous matrimonial websites, eager to expand his horizons in the search for genuine love. But this journey wasn't just about romance. His commitment to self-care triggered a profound transformation. His vitality and enthusiasm began to radiate in both his professional and personal life. Friends and colleagues noticed the change, showering him with compliments and admiration. Recognition at work followed, and his external appearance started to reflect the newfound confidence blossoming within him.

It was a moment of clarity. Vikram realised that many people went through similar journeys, some emerging stronger and others trapped in a cycle of self-doubt and suffering. This insight became his calling. He decided to share the wisdom and insights he gained through his transformation. Instagram seemed like the perfect platform—a place where countless individuals sought answers to life's challenges.

With a newfound passion for helping others, Vikram began his Instagram journey with motivational quotes. What started as a simple intention evolved into something more profound. As he shared his trials and triumphs, people from around the world reached out to him, revealing their own struggles. It hit him—people were suffering in silence, lacking the tools to navigate their challenges. This realisation, inspired by Dr. Denaz's observations on the societal silence surrounding mental health, ignited a fire within him. He wanted to shatter the stigma and demonstrate that seeking help is a brave act, not a weakness. His mission was clear: to shed light on mental wellness.

Initially, Vikram's IT background led him to consider creating an app. However, he soon understood a pivotal truth: many mental health issues stem from a lack of human connection. Digital solutions alone could make the problem worse. So, he redirected his efforts toward fostering real connections, offering a listening ear, and creating a safe space for sharing. True healing, he realised, begins with human connection, support, and breaking the silence surrounding mental health.

Vikram's transformative journey to Kedarkantha had ignited a spark within him, setting the stage for further transformation. Along the way, he encountered remarkable individuals whose guidance helped him evolve. Driven by clarity and purpose, he decided to create a blueprint for transformation, blending it with a rejuvenating retreat. Extensive research revealed a lack of mental wellness retreats, presenting a golden opportunity.

With meticulous planning, from finding the perfect location to designing an engaging event flyer, Vikram began conceptualising his mental wellness retreat. Serendipity struck when he shared his vision with an Instagram follower, a seasoned digital marketing expert. Impressed, this ally helped launch a campaign that captured many imaginations, resulting in an overwhelming response. Vikram decided to start small, with just 20 seats for the inaugural retreat. As the journey progressed, Vikram felt propelled towards his dream. This wasn't just his journey; it was an invitation for others to join him in self-discovery and growth. With each challenge, he found opportunity. As he shaped his vision, he felt a sense of excitement, knowing something extraordinary was unfolding. The adventure had just begun, and he was eager to inspire and uplift those ready to embark on this transformative journey.

Amidst the backdrop of his meticulously organised retreat, destiny had a sweet surprise. As the sun set and the campfire's glow illuminated the eager participants, his eyes met hers. She was a vision of grace and laughter, her eyes sparkling like stars. Their conversation flowed effortlessly, and their laughter was a melodious serenade. Under the night sky, their connection deepened. Sharing stories and dreams, it was clear they were kindred spirits on a similar journey of self-discovery. The campfire's flickering flames mirrored the sparks between them, signalling the beginning of a beautiful chapter in their lives. The universe seemed to have conspired to bring them together, and as they gazed at the stars, they felt the start of a remarkable love story, one that would be written in the pages of their transformational journey.

In the quiet corners of his soul, Vikram found the courage to pen the story of his transformation. As the pages turn, a promise lingers: a future, vibrant and limitless, awaits those who dare to embark on their own transformative odyssey.

****** THE END ******